24x 1/06

FISHING SPIDERS

THE SPIDER DISCOVERY LIBRARY

Louise Martin

Rourke Enterprises, Inc.
Vero Beach, Florida 32964

LIBRARY OF CONGRESS
Library of Congress Cataloging-in-Publication Data

Martin, Louise, 1955-
Fishing spiders/by Louise Martin.

p. cm. — (The Spider discovery library)
Includes index.
Summary: Describes the physical characteristics, habits, and natural environment of two kinds of fishing spiders, the North American Dolomedes triton and the European Argyroneta.
ISBN 0-86592-964-5
1. Dolomedes—Juvenile literature. 2. Argyroneta—Juvenile literature. 3. Spiders—Juvenile literature. [1. Dolomedes, 2. Argyroneta. 3. Fisher spiders. 4. Spiders.]
I. Title. II. Series:
Martin, Louise, 1955-
Spider discovery library.
QL458.42.P5M37   1988
595.4'4 - dc19   88-5967
                    CIP
                    AC

Title page photo: A fishing spider attacks a large insect

TABLE OF CONTENTS

FISHING SPIDERS

Two kinds of fishing spiders are called *Dolomedes* (do lo MED es) and *Argyroneta* (ar gyr ON et a). They are from the *Pisauridae* family of spiders. The spiders of the *Pisauridae* family are quite large and strong. They have long legs and are covered with short hairs. *Dolomedes* is dark brown with yellow markings, while *Argyroneta* is brown with a grey **abdomen**.

A fishing spider perches on a water plant

WHERE THEY LIVE

The North American fishing spider, *Dolomedes triton*, is sometimes called the six-dotted spider because of the six dark spots on its back. Other species of *Dolomedes* spiders are common in Europe, Australia, and South Africa. *Argyroneta* is found only in Northern Europe. Both *Dolomedes* and *Argyroneta* live in wet places like swamps, marshes, ponds, and lakes.

A Dolomedes triton on the surface of a pond

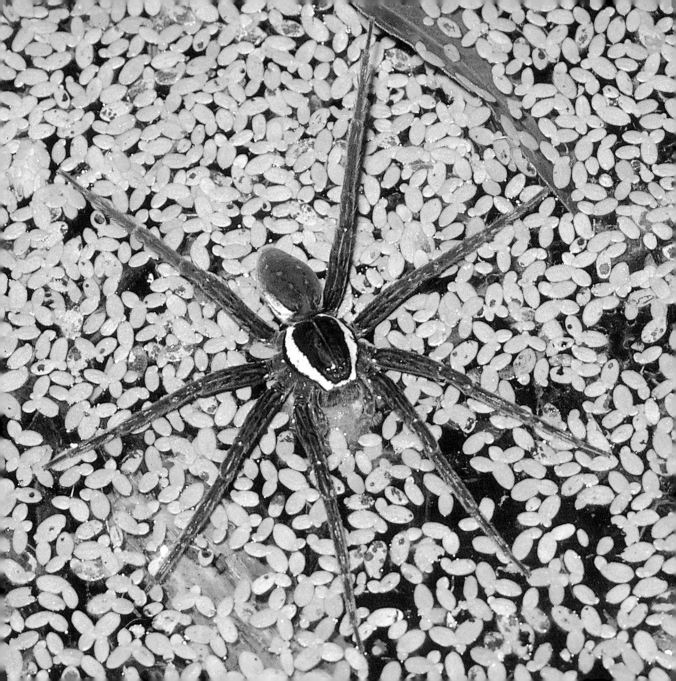

FEMALE DOLOMEDES

Female *Dolomedes* lay several batches of eggs in the summer months. Each time, they may lay a thousand eggs in two greenish-colored **sacs.** The sacs are often dipped in the water to keep them moist, otherwise the eggs become too dry and the **spiderlings** do not hatch. The female *Dolomedes* spin silk around the egg sacs. They carry the sacs under their abdomen for two or three weeks.

A female fishing spider carrying her egg sac

BABY DOLOMEDES

When the spiderlings are about to hatch from the eggs, the female *Dolomedes* carefully place the egg sacs down. They begin to spin a **nursery tent** around the sacs. The spiderlings hatch from the eggs in the safety of the tent. The mother spiders stay on guard with their young while they are in the nursery tent. When the spiderlings have **molted** twice, they are big enough to leave the tent.

A fishing spider guards her nursery tent

An Argyroneta with its be[ll]

Argyronetas live mostly underwater

LIVING UNDERWATER

Argyronetas can spend their whole lives underwater. They build a sort of diving bell as a home. First they anchor a sheet of silk to a stem or plant under the water. Then they return to the surface of the water and trap air in their abdomen. Swimming down under their silk canopy, they release the bubble of air and trap it under the silk. After a few trips down to their home with air from the surface, the bell is ready for them to live in.

A Dolomedes with its air bubble underwater

WHAT ARGYRONETAS EAT

Argyronetas live mostly on insects that they find in the water. They also eat tiny fish, fish eggs, and **tadpoles**. The spiders sit with their bodies in their "bells" and their legs in the water. They can feel the movement of fish and insects passing by. *Argyronetas* pounce quickly when they feel suitable **prey** close to them. They drag their victims back to their bells to feed.

A fishing spider dangles its feet in the water to attract insects

DOLOMEDES

Dolomedes do not remain below the surface of the water for as long as *Argyronetas*, nor do they build their homes under water. *Dolomedes* spend most of their time on the surface of the water. They are able to run easily across both water and dry land. Sometimes *Dolomedes* need to dive underwater, either in search of prey or to avoid **predators**. They trap tiny bubbles of air between the hairs on their bodies which they use to breathe when they are underwater.

A fishing spider eats a fly

DOLOMEDES' PREY

Dolomedes and *Argyronetas* never eat in the water. Like all spiders, they have to inject their prey with **venom** to **paralyze** it. If they did this underwater, the venom would become **diluted** and would not work. *Argyronetas* drag their prey to the safety of their bell, and *Dolomedes* lift their prey out of the water onto a leaf or onto dry land. There they begin to feed.

A fishing spider with her nursery web.

HOW THEY EAT

Dolomedes eat insects that fall into the ponds or swamps where they live. They normally catch them on the surface of the water. Sometimes *Dolomedes* sit on leaves in the middle of the pond, gently waving their front legs in the water. The movement of their legs attracts small fish and brings them to the surface. When a fish comes close, the spider grabs it in its strong jaws.

Glossary

abdomen (AB do men) — the back or hind part of a spider's body

dilute (di LUTE) — to make a fluid weaker by adding water

to molt (MOLT) — to shed an outer layer of skin or hair

nursery tent (NUR ser y TENT) — a silk sheet in the shape of a tent spun by female spiders to protect their eggs and babies

paralyze (PAR a lyze) — to make a person or animal unable to move

predator (PRED a tor) — an animal that hunts others for food

prey (PREY) — an animal that is hunted for food

sacs (SACS) — pouches that contain eggs

spiderlings (SPI der lings) — baby spiders

tadpoles (TAD poles) — small, black fish-like creatures that develop into frogs

venom (VEN om) — poison

INDEX